To: YANGKI
From: Tim and Da...

THE INCREDIBLY
RADICAL
BRADICAL

WRITTEN BY L.C. BAKER
ILLUSTRATED BY JEF PONKAN

Copyright © 2025 by L.C. Baker

All rights reserved.

No part of this book may be reproduced, stored in a retrieval system, or transmitted in any form or by any means (electronic, mechanical, photocopying, recording, or otherwise) without prior written permission of the copyright holder, except for brief quotations used in critical articles or reviews.

ISBN Paperback 978-1-0693218-0-0
ISBN Hardcover 978-1-0693218-1-7

First Edition 2025
Publisher: L.C. Baker
Toronto, Canada

Acknowledgments

Illustrations by Jefril Ponkan, Philippines
Edited by Jennifer McIntyre, Toronto Canada
Contractual Legal Services by Martyn Krys, Toronto Canada
Formatting and Design by Susi Clark, Creative Blueprint Design, USA
Photoshop Editing and Design Support by Paul Thomas, OSSIA Creative, Toronto Canada
Special Thanks to: Kevin Camilleri, Nolan Camilleri, Hudson Camilleri, Logan Camilleri

This book is a work of fiction. The characters, events, and settings are entirely a product of the author's imagination. Any resemblance to actual persons, living or dead, or actual events is purely coincidental.

DEDICATED TO NOLAN, HUDSON, AND LOGAN

There once was a kitty—his name was **CAT**

—Who purred and licked and window-sat.

Tuna stew is what he ate.

For every meal he ate it straight.

He wondered what was more to do,

But kept on eating tuna stew,

And window-watching was his view,

"'Cause that's what I'm **SUPPOSED** to do."

HIS NAME WAS CAT THE KITTY.

There once was a bunny—her name was **HOP**—

Who hopped so much her ears would flop.

Carrot pie was what she munched,

For breakfast, dinner and for lunch.

She wondered what was more to do,

But carrot pie was all she knew,

With floppy hopping all day through,

"'Cause that's what I'm **SUPPOSED** to do."

HER NAME WAS HOP THE BUNNY.

There once was a bird—his name was **TWEET**—

Who soared the sky from tree to tree.

He slurped and gobbled worm soufflé,

Each afternoon, each night, each day.

He wondered what was more to do,

But worm soufflé was all he'd chew.

From tree to tree he always flew,

"'Cause that's what I'm **SUPPOSED** to do."

HIS NAME WAS TWEET THE BIRD.

There once was a dog; his name was **BRADICAL.**

For short, he went by **BRAD**, all capitals.

The food he ate, it varied so,

Depending on his mood, **YA KNOW**.

He'd sometimes like a **PANCAKE** stack.

He'd always drink his **COFFEE** black.

He walked a bit, but truth be told,

A **SKATEBOARD** was his favorite mode.

And BRAD loved music, you might say.

He banged and boomed his **DRUMS** most days.

To clear your brain in case it's foggy,

BRAD was **NOT** your average doggy.

He wore a cape and **FUZZY SLIPPERS**.

He trimmed his **MULLET** with his clippers.

And though he'd sometimes fetch a ball,

You'd likely find BRAD at the **MALL**.

And for this claim, you might want references:

See, BRAD had certain

'POTTY PREFERENCES.'

So, rather than the grass, he'd choose…

A TOILET FOR HIS NUMBER TWO'S!

"ENOUGH!" cried Cat.

Hop joined in: **"REALLY?!**

"Now, this is getting awfully silly!

"A pancake-eating, skating pooch?!

"That's not what you're *supposed* to do!"

"Dogs eat kibble!" Tweet firmly said.

"Dogs drink water!" Cat shook his head.

"Dogs don't drum or roam the mall.

"Dogs spend all day chasing balls!"

"And slippers on your furry feet?!

"OH GOODNESS ME, OH MY!" cried Tweet.

Together Cat and Hop and Tweet

All stood up on their tippy feet.

They shouted loud, with no enjoyment:

"AND DOGGIES SURE CAN'T USE THE TOILET!"

"Here, here," said BRAD, "this you should know:

"I **LOVE** my morning cuppa joe.

"Pancakes are a delightful food,

"And drumming really helps my mood.

"The mall has many awesome spaces.

"My board takes me to awesome places.

"This mullet suits my furry head.

"These slippers keep me warm in bed.

"And, not to get us all a-blushing,

"**BUT I LIKE THE SOUND OF TOILETS FLUSHING!**

"So not to sound extremely sappy,

"But these are things that make me **HAPPY.**

"See, different things aren't weird or laughable.

"These different things—they make me **BRADICAL.**

"And as for **'CAN'T'** ... well, here's some truth:

"**I, MYSELF, AM LIVING PROOF!**

"So, **YOU** should try out something new.

"It just might make **YOU** happy too."

Now Cat and Hop said, "Could this be?"

"OH GOODNESS, ME OH MY," said Tweet.

"Could it be so that that BRAD—so different,

"So non-conforming, so deliberate,

"Non-typical, but quite profound,

"Might also be a **HAPPY** hound?"

Together, Cat and Hop and Tweet

All stood up on their tippy feet.

They shouted loud, their thoughts anew:
"LET'S BE OURSELVES! LET'S TRY IT TOO!"

AND CAT SOON PLANS TO GO CANOEING,
"'CAUSE THAT IS WHAT I ENJOY DOING."
HIS NAME IS CAT THE KITTY.

café

THERE LIVES A BUNNY. HER NAME IS HOP.
SHE LISTENS TO DISCO, RAP AND POP.

SHE LOVES TO DANCE AND SHE'S LEARNED TO STAND.
SHE IS THE SINGER IN HER BAND.

Hop plans to go hot-air ballooning, "cause that is what I enjoy doing." Her name is Hop the Bunny.

THERE LIVES A BIRD. HIS NAME IS TWEET.
HE'S EARNED TWO MEDALS IN HIS HEAT.
HE LEADS A LOCAL RUNNING GROUP,
AND SLURPS A HEARTY SPINACH SOUP.

And Tweet soon plans to go snowshoeing, "cause that is what I enjoy doing." His name is Tweet the Bird.

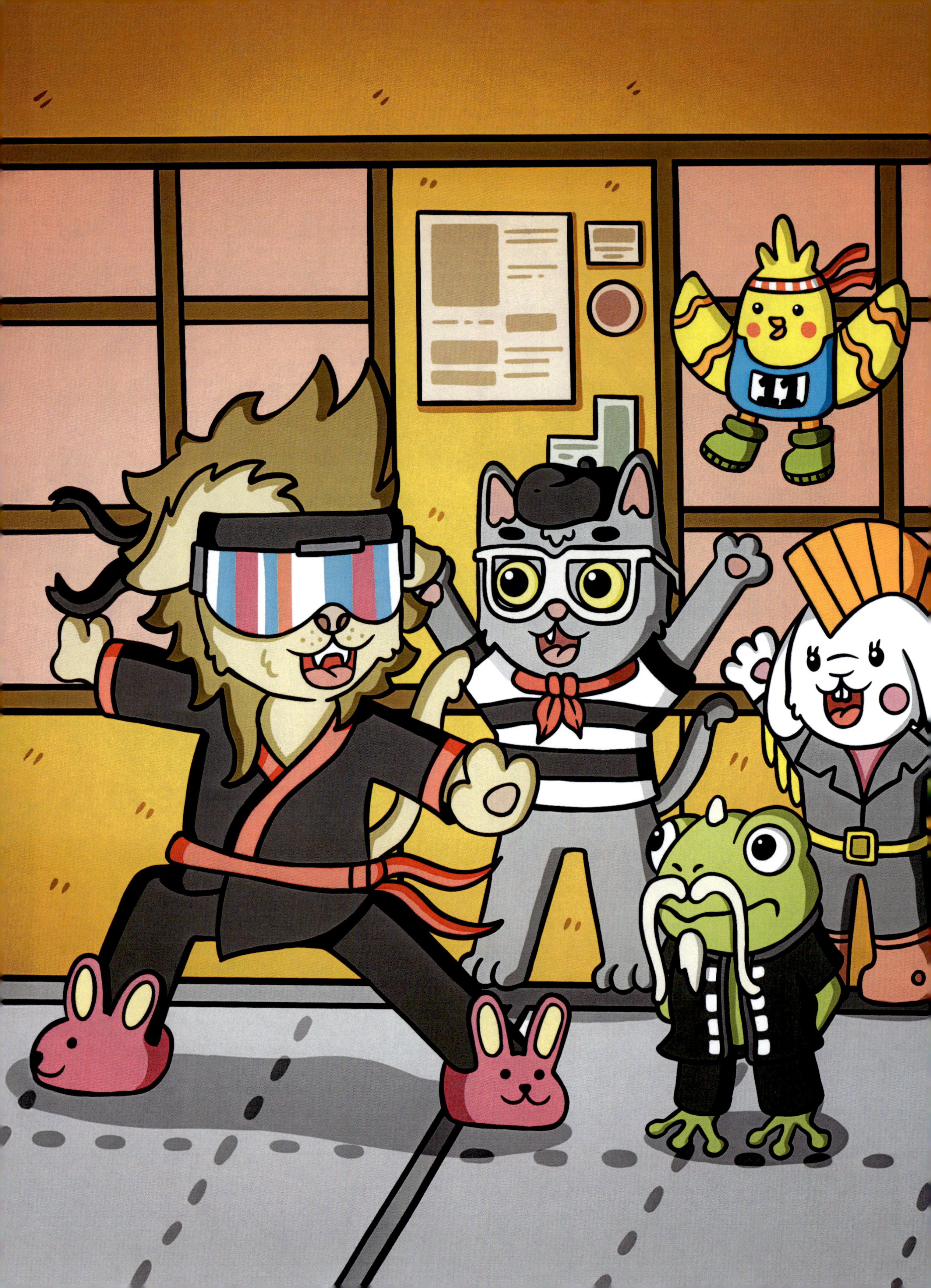
11

And as for BRAD? **HE LEARNED KUNG FU!**

He's made new friends,

And **HELPED** some too.

BUT...

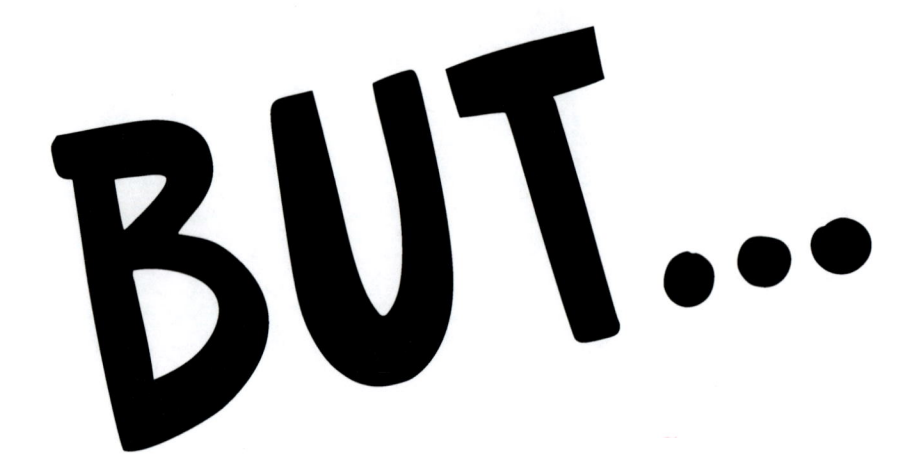

There's one more item on his list.

See, BRAD is **VERY** curious…

So listen close and think these through,

For these questions all are meant for…

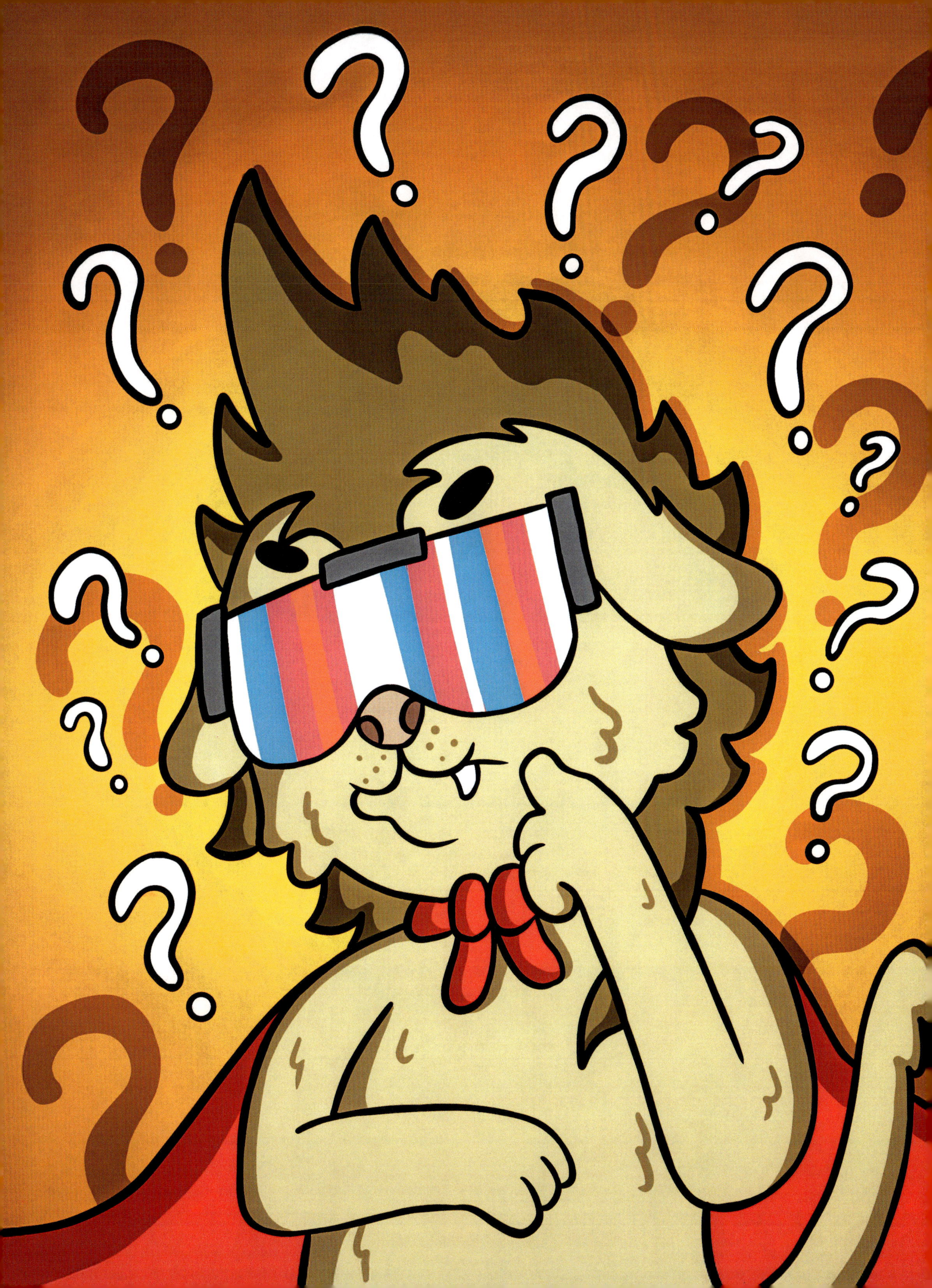

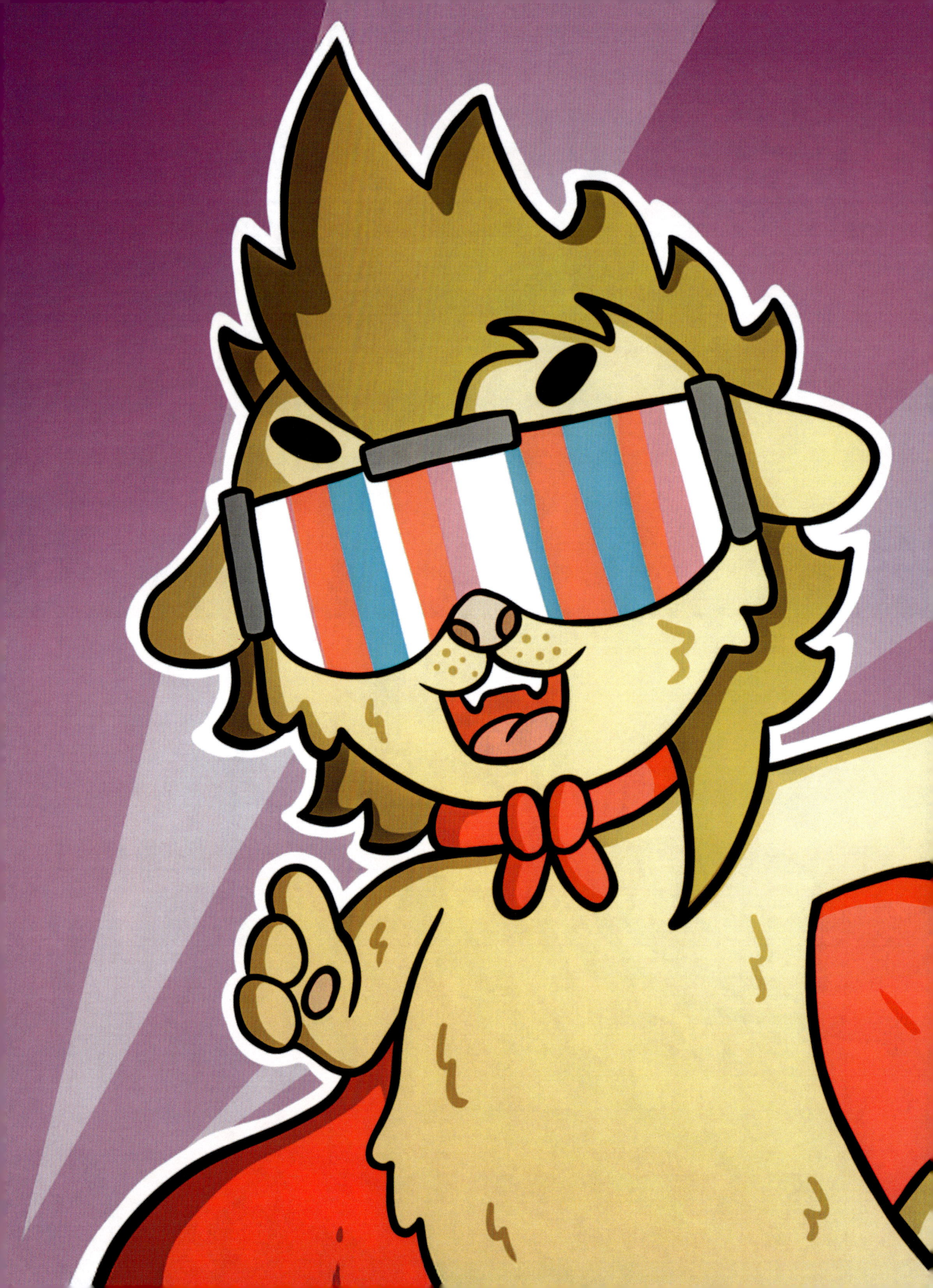

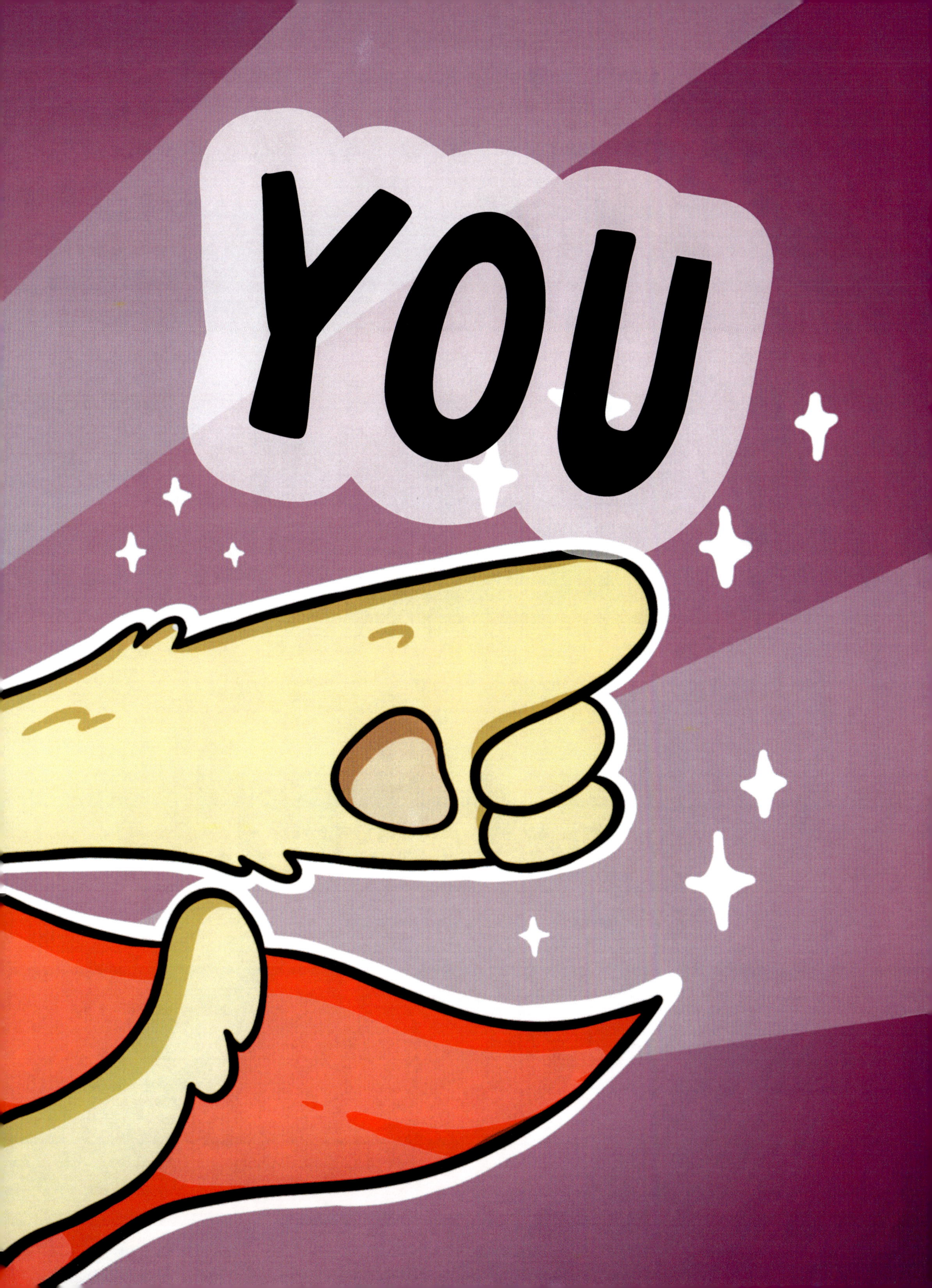
YOU

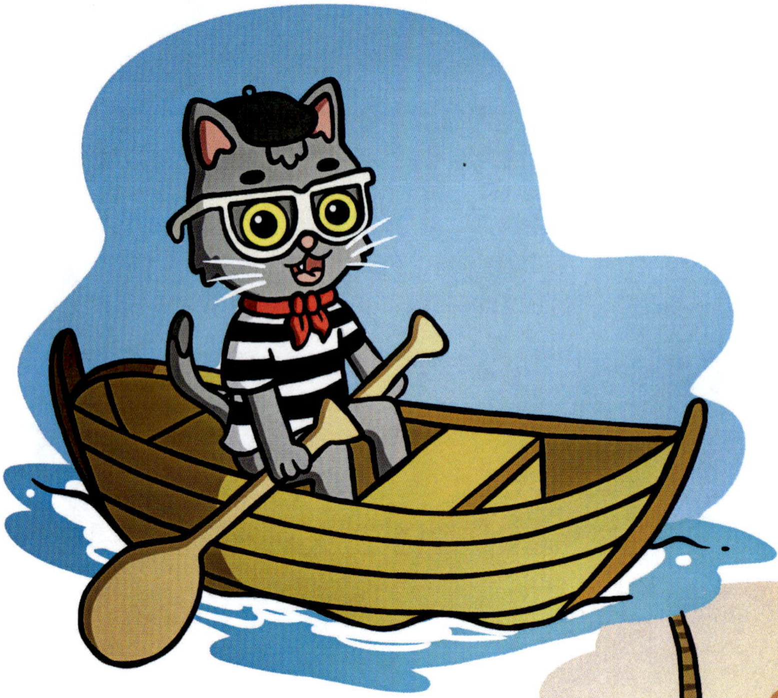

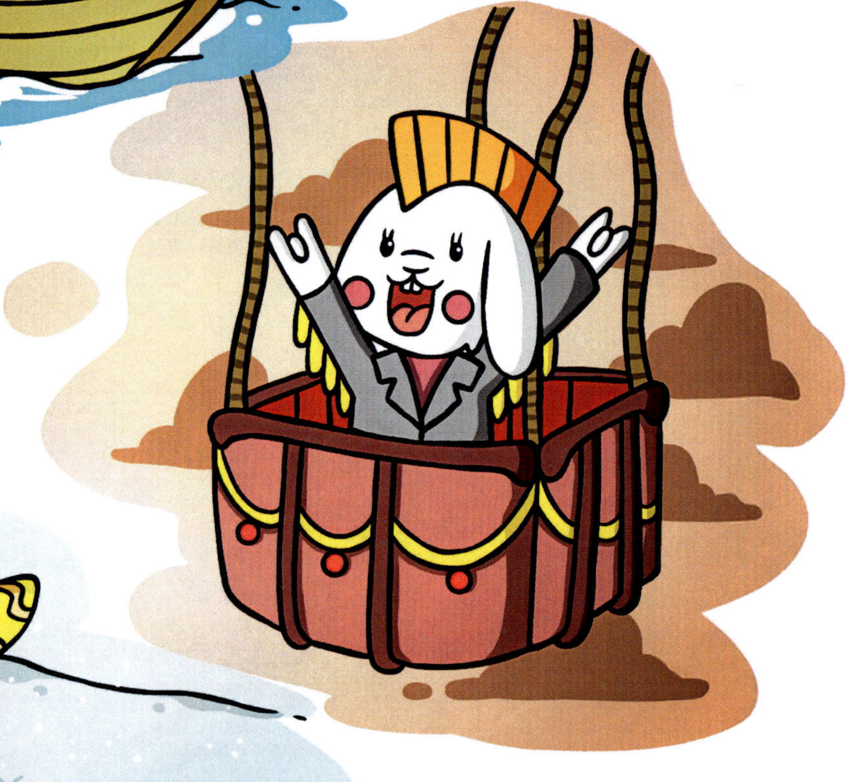

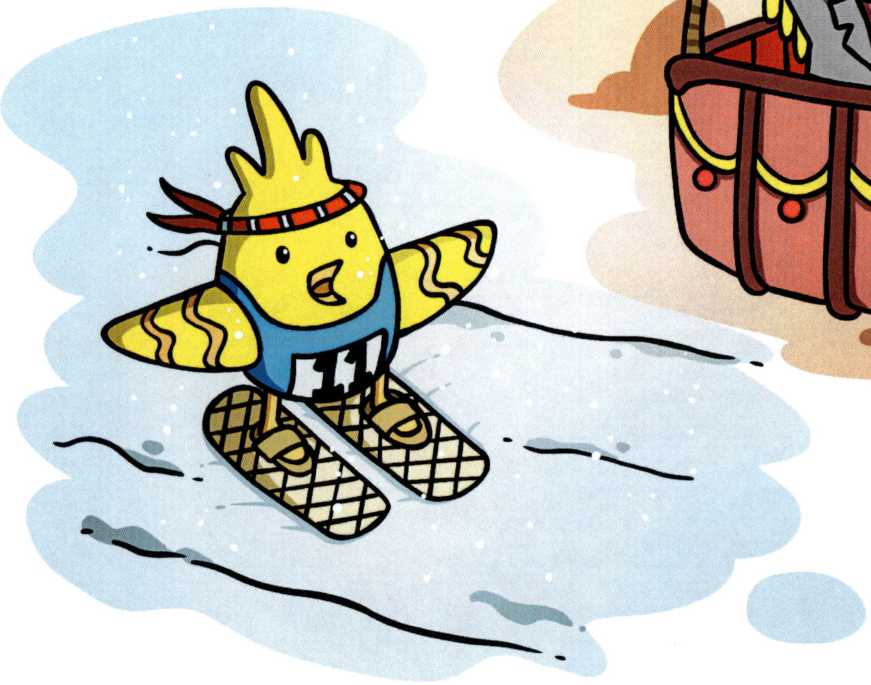
11

What is **YOUR** name?

What do **YOU** do?

And what exactly makes **YOU, YOU?**

There is no right or wrong to these,
There never was **SUPPOSED** to be.

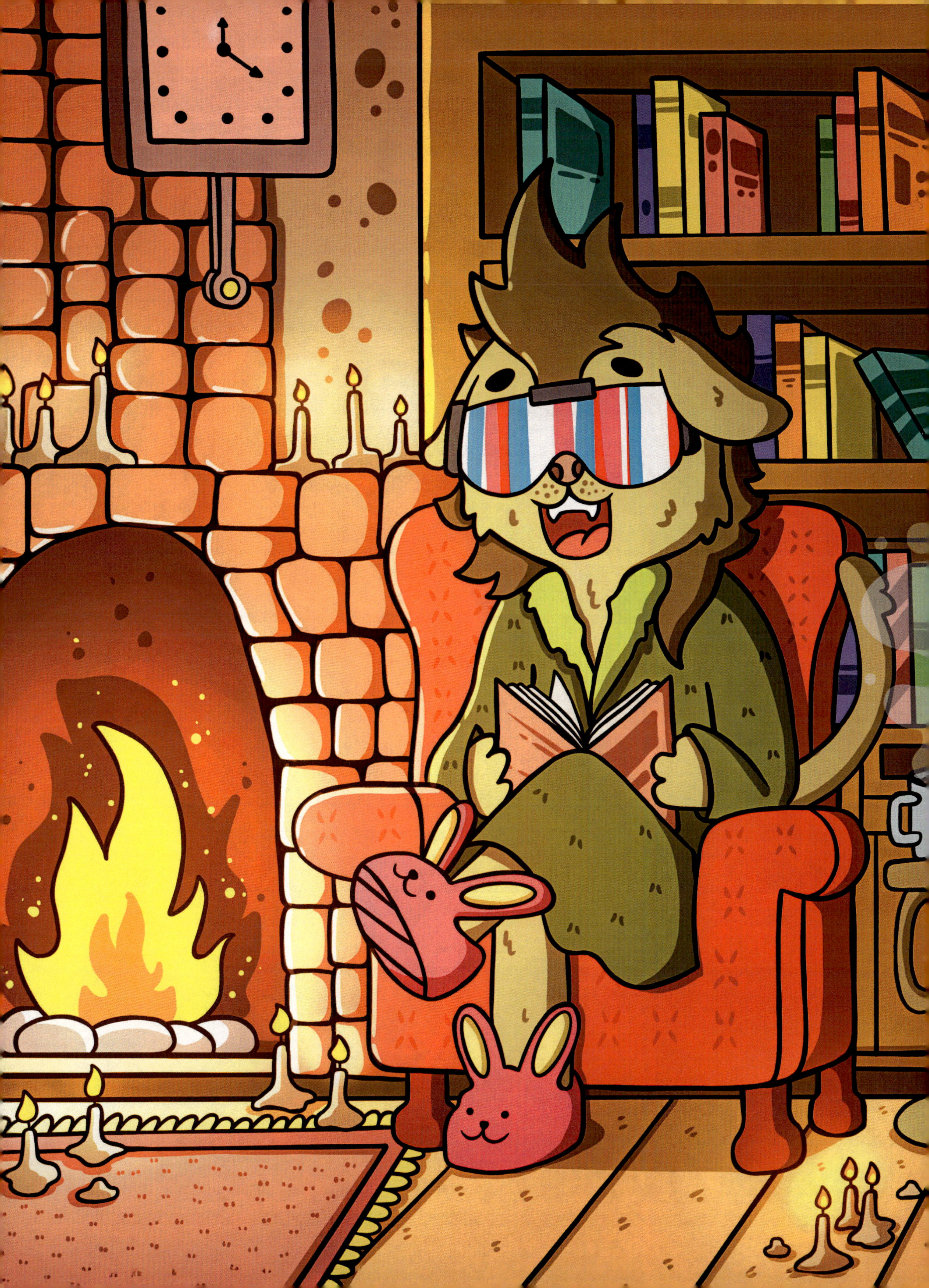

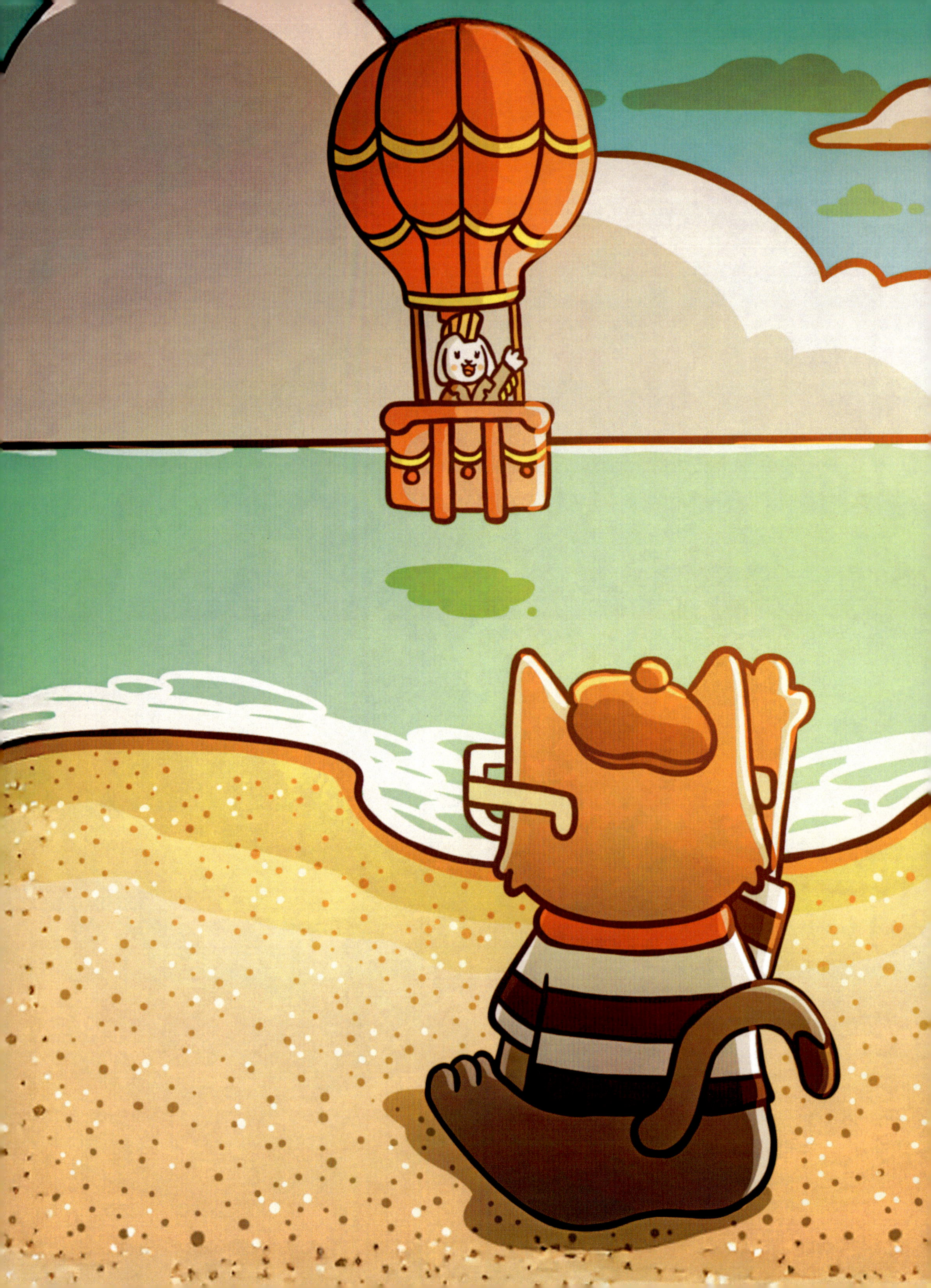

So **BE YOURSELF,** AND YOU'LL GO FAR. YOU'RE PERFECT **JUST THE WAY YOU ARE.**

THE END

Manufactured by Amazon.ca
Acheson, AB